Wipe clean
Read and Write

When you see a book, read
the words aloud.

When you see a pen, trace over the
words with a felt-tip pen.

When you see a dotted line, copy
the correct word onto it.

Ladybird

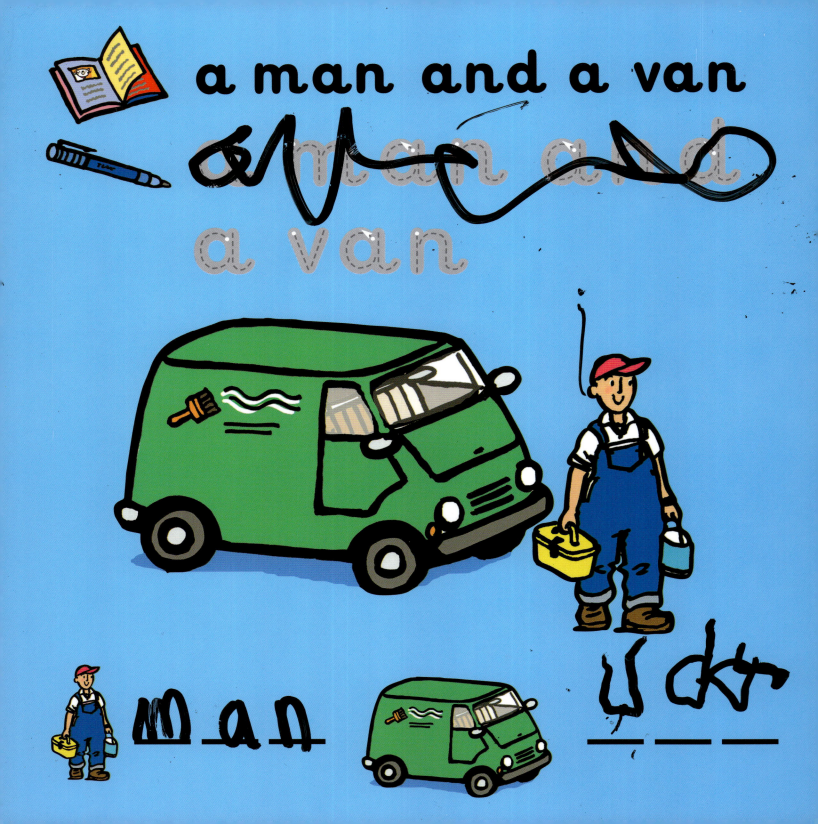

a man and a van

a man and

a van

man

a cat and a hat

a fox in a box

a fox in
a box

 — — — —  — — — —

a dog in a fog

a dog in
a fog

_ _ _ _   _ _ _ _

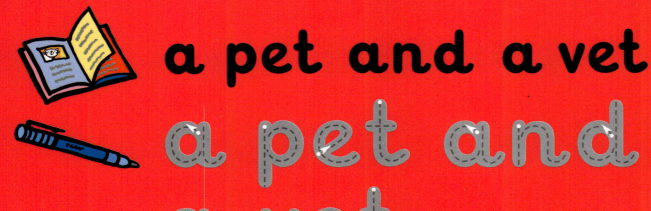

a pet and a vet

a pet and
a vet

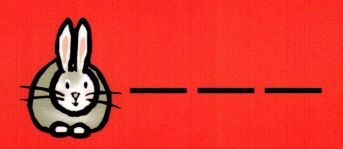 _ _ _ _ _ _

 _ _ _

a hen and a pen

a hen and
a pen

 _ _ _  _ _ _

a pig in a wig

a pig in
a wig

 _ _ _ _  _ _ _ _

a tin in a bin

a tin in a bin

 _ _ _  _ _ _

a cub in a tub

a cub in a tub

 _ _ _ _  _ _ _ _

a bull in a bus

a bull in a bus

 _ _ _ _ _  _ _ _ _ _

a fish on a dish

a fish on a dish

 — — — — — —  — — — — — —

a sock on a rock

a sock on a rock

 — — — — — — — —  — — — — — —

a king and a ring

a king and
a ring

_ _ _ _ _ _ _ _

a band in the sand

a band in the sand

Practise writing...

a b c d e f

g h i j k l m

n o p q r s t

u v w x y z